For Ju

Best w...

Sinéad Coxhill

Menopausal Mermaids & Life Lines

By

Sinéad Coxhill

impspired@gmail.com

Cover designed by Karen Maguire

Illustrations by P. Mullan

ISBN: 978-1-915819-37-6

To Michael
for shared times
and shared poetry

OTHER TITLES BY IMPSPIRED

Each Imaginary Arrow –
by Scott Ferry

Rueful -
by Kathleen Denizard

The Bones of the Story –
by Sandra Arnold

Magic Cube of Time -
by Vatsala Radhakeesoon

Fractured Echoes –
by Geraldine Fleming

Children of the Storm –
by Ann Christine Tabaka

Karma Cola –
by Pranab Ghosh

IMPSPIRED

Introduction

Sinéad Coxhill began writing poetry in 2014. Until recently some of her work was languishing in notebooks. In 2022 she began to gather her poetry together with a view to publishing a collection. The title she chose was *Menopausal Mermaids & Life Lines*. She divided the work into five sections reflecting different parts of her life. Growing up on a farm in Northern Ireland she has written about both her parents and her childhood experience. Her hope is that these poems will speak particularly to those who have had a similar rural upbringing both in Northern Ireland and further afield. She lives in the north coast town of Portrush. The sea is central to her life. A sea swimmer she also walks by the sea daily. One of the five strands of the book is comprised of poems about her relationship with the sea. Belonging to a group of sea swimmers called the Menopausal Mermaids she is proud to be part of this fun-loving and brave group of women who swim daily throughout the year. They have inspired three of her poems as well as the title of her collection.

Another part of the collection holds her reflections on the rawness of loss and bereavement, and about reaching a degree of accommodation to that loss.

The fourth segment came from Sinéad's inner child, and presents the reader with poetry in that child's voice as well as some short fantasy stories for children of all ages. The final section contains those poems which she wanted to include but she felt did not fit into any of the other niches.

Her wish is that you, the reader enjoy this collection.

Acknowledgements

The poems and prose pieces in this collection have been written over the past eight years. I would like to express my sincere thanks to the individuals and groups who have supported me in my writing during that time.

I particularly wish to thank creative writing group facilitators, Kate Murphy and Mary Farrell for their encouragement and assistance. This book would not have come to fruition without Mary's hard work, commitment and patience.

Thanks to Portrush Writers and North Coast Writers for their nurturing and feedback over the years. It has been such a pleasure to be a member of both groups.

To help craft my writing I participated in workshops led by many excellent writers who inspired and enriched my work. At the risk of overlooking someone I will single out just two for special mention, Bernie McGill and Lemn Sissay both inspired me greatly.

Finally, grateful thanks to the following:

- to Steve Cawte, editor of Impspired.com for his support and editing expertise.
- to Judith Anderson for proof reading.
- to Northern Ireland artist, Karen Maguire for her beautiful cover design.
- to Northern Ireland artist, P. Mullan for his wonderful illustrations.

- to Jim Brolly for his invaluable technical support.

Creativity does not flourish in a vacuum. Thank you all for walking on my path with me.

REVIEWS

By Jimmy Milliken, Author of Cracking the Air, (Impspired 2022)

In this collection Sinead Coxhill takes us from childhood days in rural Ulster to life today on the North Coast. And with an added bonus, for they are interspersed with some delightful stories for children.

The poems are at times raw, at times tender, always lyrical. Sometimes they can seem simple and almost childlike but this is a deception, for within they reveal a poignancy and a melancholy, but also an exuberant joy for life. There is too a reverence for the beauty of the natural world, and an awe for the sheer power of natural forces. They are poems which demand to be read and read again… and again, and within each reading we may receive a glimpse of wisdom and profound truths.

The poems deal with a myriad of subjects: pain and heartache, sorrow and loss, but also there is love, a deep respect of nature and the pure exhilaration that nature brings to us. The language is sparse, concise and yet it rings and sings. The poems are down to earth and yet at times almost touched with enchantment. Suddenly within the reading of a poem we will discover a phrase that seems to reach into the very heart of things.

Reader, take this collection to your heart! Don't skim through it! Instead take each poem for what it is: a precious gem to be held and gazed at again and again. For within is beauty, reverence and wonder.

By Mary Farrell, Facilitator of North Coast Writers Group, Author of *It's Like Walking a Tightrope* (2021), *Out of the Chrysalis* (2022), *The Kingdom* (2022), *Springboards* (2022). All published by Impspired

Rarely have I read a book with such a true Voice. Each of its five strands reveals more and more about the Writer in the most compelling way. When 'the sea sings', we are beside her when she walks along beaches, gazes at different seascapes throughout the year, and allows us to share in her exhilaration when immersed in, and nourished by, the oceans power. But what else has created this uniquely pure Voice? When 'the farm smiled', we discover the roots and bedrock from which she came, on which she grew - her family, the land, the rhythms of the farming year and the charm of a more innocent time when children were allowed to play with a free rein. Then the Author 'heart shares' and brings us into her core. We learn of her joys and her pain, her loves and her losses. We feel privileged to stand by her side at such intimate moments. But there's still more. We are allowed to share in her survival, her ability to retain her inner child's voice, her tenacity in holding onto magic. When 'her child says', we listen with enchantment, and like Bobby, close this part of the book with a smile, our own inner selves nourished. With 'afterwords', just when we feel this Writer could have no more to reveal, such an array of perceptions, such insights into human dynamics.

The Collection leaves the reader humbled at this Writer's honesty, her forthrightness. We are inspired to read its pages again and again, trusting that the purity of these poems will shed light on our own lives. We can only learn and grow through many many readings of this unique Collection.

By Geraldine Fleming, Co- Leader of North Coast Writers Group, Author of *Curiosity* (2023) and *Fractured Echoes* (2023). Both published by Impspired.

This gentle collection celebrates life in all its subtleties and guises. Delicately crafted poems and short stories invite us to explore the poet's deep relationship with heart and home. Presented across five sections this pure and honest voice assembles connections between family, place, love, loss and precious nostalgia. Woven deftly through life's personal joys and sorrows are moments of resilience, vivid sparks of reflection.

The restorative presence of the sea and observations on seaside life serve as a reminder of the physical and emotional benefits gifted by nature and the Menopausal Mermaids. Snapshots of country life and childhood memories portray an affinity with familial closeness and reveal the source of inner strength.

This heartfelt collection resonates with a talent for observing the small details in life, capturing these unique moments in time and, in sharing them, declaring their significance.

By Kate Murphy, storyteller and facilitator, a regular contributor to My story on BBC Radio Ulster, editor for Portrush Writers of four collections of poetry and short stories.

These are poems from someone who knows the sea in all its moods, whether it is "hurling itself violently against the sea wall" or is "coyly calm, slightly ruffled by the wind". But this poet is more than just a watcher. She is immersed in the sea, "skin sandpapered by the elements" and cherishes the privilege of sharing the element with seals and dolphins.

There is a section which captures the essence of the seaside town in which she lives – a town which is packed away with the carousel at the end of the season and the sun is "wrapped in tissue paper" as autumn rolls into winter. Covid menace hangs over the poem, "Portrush Prom 2020". "Lowry's stick men…promenade" and "a watery sun feebly fights clouds / while a grey army blanket of mist / slowly rolls across the sand."

Sinead is equally at home when writing about her early life on the home farm. We are treated to images of milking time when the "milk squirts its rhythm into the bucket" and of the tilly lamp that "hisses like a boiling kettle". While the detail of the killing and preparing of the chicken for Sunday dinner might convert the hardest carnivore to vegetarianism, the apple pie, "sweet, spicy, sensuous, sugared, cloved", tantalises the taste buds.

Most poignant perhaps are the poems about grief, the grief of losing parents, and especially of the mourning a child for "the life [he] did not have". "Words are wholly inadequate to convey grief's depths", but nevertheless the poet finds "a sense of peace in the presence of greatness."

The poems in the child's voice and the short stories are fun, to be enjoyed by children, or by the child in all of us. This collection has much that we all can empathise with. It has something for everyone, so do yourself a favour, put the kettle on, cut a slice of cake, sit down with this book and take time to enjoy Sinead's wonderful collection.

CONTENTS

~ and the sea sang ~

24 - Menopausal Mermaids
27 - Creator
28 - Portrush in Autumn
29 - Jackson Pollock Beach
30 - Sharing the Sea
31 - Murmuration
32 - Today I Miss the Sea
33 - Mad or Brave
34 - West Strand
35 - Seaside Rituals
36 - Scene of Crime
37 - Gift
38 - The Ocean Siren
40 - Seascapes
41 - Portrush Prom 2020
42 - April
43 – Seagull

~ and the farm smiled ~

45 - Baking Day
47 - Milking Time
49 - The Tilley Lamp
50 - The Ritual
52 - Apple Pie
53 - Ageing
55 - Byre

56 - Turas Deireanach
58 - Grain of Sand
59 - Talismans
60 - Stones
61 - Lough Derg
63 - Intruder
64 - Prayer
65 - Photos
66 - Flight
68 - The Jumper
69 - Charlie

~ and the heart shares ~

71 - Fragility
72 - Hugh
73 - Stillness
75 - Jack
76 - Incantation
77 - You

~ and the child said ~

79 - The Magic Box
81 - A Watery Adventure
87 - Hortense the Giraffe
89 - The Elf on the Shelf
92 - The Stone Seal
94 - An Unlikely Hero
96 - The Amazing Abel Starlight
103 - Kiss Chase

104 - War
105 - Closeness
106 - Russell Park, London
107 - Skipping
108 - Disco
109 - Butterfly
110 - The Magic Box (II)

~ afterwords ~

113 - Balm
114 - Zendo
115 - Saving
116 - Synaestheses
118 - Transition
119 - I Don't Really Need You Now
120 - Let There Be Laughter
121 - Twenty-one
122 - I Come From
124 - Acknowledgements of First Publication
127 - Notes
129 - About the Author

~ and the sea sang ~

Menopausal Mermaids

November

meeting early morning
beneath a crepuscular sky
striding into the sea
chill wind on my shoulders
ankle deep in cold water

wondering as always
about finding courage
for immersion
I walk further out until
my legs are wet
scooping handfuls
splashing myself

coldness almost takes
my breath away
friends dive into breakers
sleek seals
I'm not so brave
staying closer to the shore
diluting waves power

December

an excoriating winter morning
we Mermaids assemble
forces of nature
quickly shedding
leggings and dry robes
rushing across the sand
wind at our backs

ten minutes in the water
laughing, hollering
diving through waves
cold air on our bodies
dashing back to dress
rapidly robing up
peeling off swimsuits

skin sand- papered
by the elements
glowing ember red
hot-cold
blood pumps
through our veins

we share our love for life
friends in Atlantic power

January

we chip ice off waves
and blow frost from surf
bodies
beyond shock
exposed to elements
speech from frozen lips
lost in white clouds

laughter
sound of seals at play
diving through waves
bodies
pulverised
afire
by foaming water

See you tomorrow
we call like sirens

Creator

his knees resting
in buff sand
I honour his artisan hands
shaping
creating

I wish his dolphin
could live   dive
tumble through waves
this fragile beauty ambered
in immobile perfection

Portrush in Autumn

the Carousel is packed away
sea folded with care in a drawer
sand brushed into neat piles
sun wrapped in tissue paper
mournful rain dampens townsfolk shoulders
holiday makers stacked on shelves
streets miss their jostling
struggle to accept autumnal quiet
crisp Autumn rolls into cold damp Winter
bright Spring foretells the promise of Summer
when the seaside will be unpacked once more

Jackson Pollock Beach

I walk the strand
poetry whispering
like soft music
with volume low
waves echo a backdrop
to memory

lone walkers   dog walkers
couples   joggers
actors on the beach
a Jackson Pollock canvas
of footprints   paw marks
hoof prints   scratch marks

wind whipped tears
        my eyes weep
            I strive to walk

Sharing the Sea

large   limpid eyes
meet my gaze
whiskers wobble
his round glossy head
mirrors our rubber caps

does he wonder at the
pink   yellow and blue
at neoprene gloved hands
like small flippers?

he watches
then slowly swims away
we cherish the privilege
of sharing his world

Murmuration

silver   scintillating sea
   like poured solder

I think of the word
   murmuration

it perfectly conjures
   the music of gentle waves

it's decided
   it's been re-invented

Today I Miss the Sea

today I miss the sea
too cold and squally
to brave the walk
in Parka and boots
squeamishly sequestered
snuggled in the warmth
made soft by smiling weather
of the last two weeks

today I miss the sea
and wonder how she seems
is she hurling herself violently
against the sea wall
or is she coyly calm
only slightly ruffled by the wind

today I miss the sea

Mad or Brave

With nervous fluttering feelings
on my walk to the sea
knowing that I'll soon enter
body shocking coldness
I size up the waves
gauging height and ferocity

the same familiar faces
seasoned dog walkers
exchange *Hellos*
an elderly man doffs his cap
calls out his comment
mad or brave

euphoric with endorphins
I journey home
with a bounce in my step
smile at the mothers
steering empty pushchairs
their toddlers careening gleefully on the prom

we share each other's buoyant joy

West Strand

walk along West Strand
glistening glimmering on water
wind a friendly cupped hand
in the small of my back
urging me forward

practice meditation
waves acting as sound track
quickly am distracted
unable to live in moment

a lone woman swims
brave no wet suit
people smile in afternoon sunshine
after a morning of relentless rain

Seaside Rituals

never said those words
We're off to the seaside
but would appear
in that blue shirt
and sunglasses
handsome
like a famous singer

fifteen miles away
drive takes forever
but is rewarded by excitement
of final downhill sweep to beach

tee shirts   shorts   sandals
are shed for that first
frenzied rush into surf

taking turns bobbing
through waves on daddy's shoulders
staying in till skin
turned blue and teeth chattered

mammy   attempting to sunbathe
complaining loudly as we
dripped seawater over her

ignoring sand crunch
of egg sandwiches
we chomped on them   ravenous

time to go home
waiting to do it all again

Scene of Crime

unusual
red and white tape
billowing on the beach
houses a lone tern
resting on the sand
statue still
ill or injured

walkers pause
photograph it
I move on
image grafted
onto my mind
like sensitive skin
will the bird survive?

on return
tape blowing in breeze
bird prone on sand
feel moved
to have shared
in its last
hour of life

I wonder if it
had suffered
was aware
my thoughts run on
how interconnected
all creatures are
in our frailty

Gift

Swimmers bask
floating free til
in a welcomed broken peace
excited dolphins dive
pirouette and smile

gasps   amazement
from the swimmers   paddlers
sunbathers on the sand
witnessing the unexpected
a dolphin spectacular

applause breaks out
somersaulting higher
they respond with joy
an audience feels blest
at a gift freely bestowed

The Ocean Siren

exchanging my warm room
for the windy chambered beach
sky-sea melds into a single grey
broken by a forlorn gull
rotting seaweed

assails my nostrils
in a sudden downpour
my body pummelled by gusts
the ocean siren calls me
timorous at first

then emboldened I immerse
brine bleeds into my tongue
as a wave swallows me
coldness steals my voice
words leak out in a ragged rasp

sea by turn
a turbulent lover
gripping me in an iron embrace
an atlantic mother
to whom I return
re-tying the umbilical cord
I feel sticky spiciness

enfolding my body
when I take my leave again
endorphins coursing
every cell reborn

I will burst forth in tomorrow's
beckoning waters

Seascapes

the sea in its palette of greens
is painted into my memory

shucking of lapping waters
over pebbles and shells

waves glide   formation dancers
seaweed strewn   cassette ribbons

a solitary beach walk
but never really alone

vertiginous waters   lowering sky
sudden downpour scours breakers
each is rinsed   renewed

I open my lips
swallow wind and rain
to experience all inside me

Portrush Prom 2020

Assailed nostrils   seaweed tang
waves taken hostage
by Lowry's stick men
bodies black clad
dogs   cyclists   prams
procure promenade

water boom echoes
I dissolve into resonance
gulls wail melding - a symphony
big wheel melts into anaemic sky
Babushka   Koko blank shutters
no clattering crockery   coffee chatter

everything disintegrating   formless
watery sun feebly fighting clouds
while a grey army blanket of mist
slowly rolls across sand

dog walker   high vis jacket
rare colour splash
houses emerge from penumbra
negative in developing fluid
then once again obliterated
an Alice *in Wonderland* illusion

April

wind scoured beach
white horses rearing
a blink of sun
brightens the mood

the helter-skelter
and big wheel
sit with gloomy gaze
on turbulent water

a dog bounces in surf
the struggling jogger pushes on
suspended far out to sea
clouds promise rain

Seagull

plaintive call   sea-synonymous
icon of the beach
yet a scavenger   opportunistic pest
sandwich thief from hapless tourists

your cries carry me back
to childhood excitement
surfing dunes
down to the shore

in Winter in a lonely seascape
you hold sea-tears in your caw
despite your bad press
I will always defend you

~ and the farm smiled ~

Baking Day

I love to watch you work
flour   margarine   buttermilk
find their way into the bowl
without any measuring
known by instinct and experience
I feel delight in watching
the bread take shape
with a clapping sound
turned patted
between deft hands

the Rayburn burns brightly
with turf and coal
racing to reach
the right temperature
for soda bread baking
you stand in the kitchen
the windows open
expelling excess heat
bright spots of colour in cheeks
your curls dishevelled

the griddle creates a bed
on which hot scones can rest
while the oven welcomes
in the loaves
a few hours more the kitchen's full
of mouth-watering bread aroma
wheaten loaves repose on trays

scones lean slant- heavy for support
shrouded in steaming cloths

Milking Time

in the twilight gloom of the byre
I watch my mother as she milks
her head rests against the cow's flank
eyes closed   transported
the steam from our two milkers
infuses the cool building

the milk squirts it's rhythm
into a bucket
an occasional swish of a tail
a thud of hooves against stone
as a cow shifts position
can I help with the milking

doubtful about the strength
of nine - year - old hands
she yields to unrelenting persuasion
with a short lesson
how to hold and squeeze the teats
to draw down the milk

all goes well
then….
without even knowing
my offence
a sudden kick lands me

                    in a gully of cow dung
it is the end of my milking career

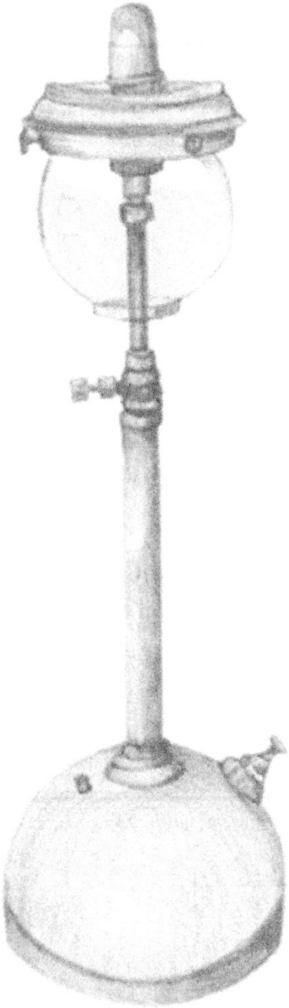

The Tilley Lamp

on those evenings
when the storms came beating
stealing away the electricity
my mother brought out the Tilley lamp
and set to pumping paraffin

a pungent smell filled the room
the lamp hissing like a boiling kettle
bathed in its bright white light the kitchen
held us all in a protective circle

sneaking away from the light
climbing the stairs in the darkness
I would slip into my bedroom
press my nose against the glass
see the sky lit with lightning

my mother would summon me back
to the safety of the white-gold circle
without TV to entertain   we played cards
my father teaching us to play whist

I cherish those memories of the Tilley lamp
but still love the power of thunderstorms

The Ritual

I loathe the ritual of Saturday morning. Donning her old apron and wellies my mother goes out to the stable where she keeps chickens for fattening.

Quickly making a selection, she pulls its neck, deftly dispatching it in a single swift move. The next half hour is a time of meditatively plucking its feathers, her eyes exhibiting a faraway look. Task complete, the bird is carried to the kitchen in its denuded state.

Pouring methylated spirits on the tiles – a pure, purple, puddle - sets fire to it. The blue flame weaves, dances. Fowl held over flame, stubborn quills are singed off. My nose smarts with the smell, but worse is still to come…

The kitchen floor is covered with sheets of newspaper. Taking her sharp knife she cuts off the head and feet, letting them drop onto it. The process of gutting begins. Discarding the putrid smelling entrails, the heart, neck and gizzard are set aside for Monday's soup.

Guts, feet and head are wrapped in an extra layer of newspaper. I am instructed to throw them in the midden. Tiptoeing across the yard with my rank parcel, I dread contact with my skin from the slimy contents, holding it away from myself like an unexploded bomb. Making the journey without incident.

On Sunday afternoon the kitchen is filled with a delicious roasting smell. Eventually my mother emerges pink and proud, the fragrant fowl centrepiece to her table.

I always feel a twinge of guilt when its smell and taste beguile me, but not enough to spoil my appetite.

Apple Pie

mellow golden brown fruit
stewed sublime
patiently waits on the counter

the pastry prepared
a yellow ground sheet rolled below
a canopy of protection
capping above

the top and bottom pinched together
in a pretty ruff
a ballet dancer's tutu of perfection

masterpiece is left to rest in hot oven
sweet   spicy   fills the kitchen
a tang   sensuous   sugared   cloved
with a flourish my mother taps crust
a secret smile hovers
she admires her peerless pie

Ageing

then:
eggs deftly packed
by wrinkled hands
she delights in her work
seventy years of farming
hard to believe

three years on:
shuffling morose
round the kitchen
on a Zimmer frame
she announces to her children
I'm useless

leafing through 'Woman's Weekly'
eyes unfocused
losing a story started
minutes earlier

care workers act as
punctuation marks
mornings – washing her
afternoons – fixing lunch
teatimes – dressing for bed

during the evenings
soaps are the diversion
from monotony
but she dozes   misses
the dramatic scenes

soon it'll be time to turn
the light out

Byre

a musky parlour
its walls holding bovine memories
the delicate aroma
of a foaming milk spray
strikes metal buckets

hair tufts adhere
to hewn stone
recalling gentle lowing
as sandpaper tongues
seek meal troughs

mother's milking days now gone
the byre's become a shed
coal   logs   instead of churns
recollections fading
like aged cobwebs

Turas Deireanach

together we watch with care
groans rumble deep within you
we talk and hold your hands
attempt to soothe
wondering if our words reach

at times peaceful
at others you struggle
you make it through the night

I wonder if this twilight state
will last
I go home to sleep
miss your final moments

in the coffin
you don't look like yourself
over the chink of teacups
neighbours chatter

the funeral morning brings torrents
like clichéd tears
sons, brothers, nephews, grandsons
step up to carry you on your way
their last act of kindness

my eyes fill
as neighbours in the deluge
line the cortege route
at the graveside the grandchildren weep

I am dry eyed
numbed as the coffin is lowered
it is your completion

yet for us life continues with
the centre of our family gone
we mourn our orphaned state
with no queen bee to our drones

Grain of Sand

I carry you with me

you are a grain of sand
waves washing over me
seaweed tangling round my feet

you are power of surfers
a concentration of castle builders
girl whizzing past on a scooter

you are cows calling to their calves
bull strutting proud
a fox in the hen house

you are a ladybird flexing its wings
a nettle which stings my hand
wind-blown dandelion seed on my face

you are a blizzard obstructing everything
a chink of light as darkness disappears
nebulous rainbow, a half arc missing

you are all places,
all times, all seasons,
you are the world

I carry you with me

Talismans

now that you are gone
objects are imbued with significance
small things belonging to everyday existence

the heavy wooden mirror
you sat before on a Saturday afternoon
rolling your curlers for Sunday Mass

your powder compact
gave you that gentle pink glow
when abroad in the outside world

brown slippers with sturdy soles
in which you sliped on your Zimmer
look now to still contain your feet

some might argue   detritus of a life
but to me they are talismans
holding magical power

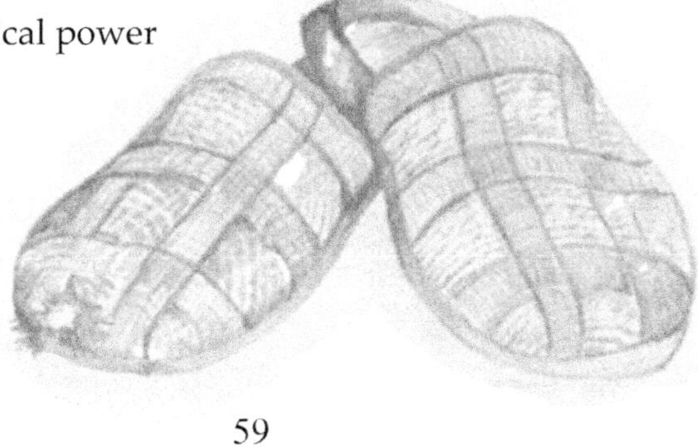

Stones

It is the job I detest most. Daddy ploughs and we are tasked with gathering the unearthed stones. He harrows and we set too again.
The tractor's link box is a voracious mouth into which all are fed. Working like convicts – seeing no progress.
Stones litter every side. Labouring until my back screams wondering if there's a point.
Season moves on   delicate re-seeded grass appears. I admire the new smoothness birthed from my heroic struggle.

Lough Derg

my father
made his pilgrimage
to Lough Derg twenty- nine times
when I was sixteen we went together
for my first and only time
and his final one…
his last year of good health
for me less a spiritual experience
than the endurance of hardship
perhaps that is a spiritual experience

it was August   raining and raw
bare feet   slipping on stones
chanting decades of the rosary
struggling with hunger -
only one meal of black toast
sleep deprived
I was tested in the chapel
as altar boys
tasked with waking sleepers
prodded me awake

my father   a seasoned pilgrim
was sympathetic but
took all sacrifices in his stride
used them to deepen his prayer

once home   to pass the time
until I could eat freed from my penance
it was straight to the parish disco
where to divert my hunger
I shared a cigarette
with midnight just chimed
nothing has ever tasted better
than the steak   eggs   tinned creamed rice
which broke my fast

Lough Derg survived
our shared privation
offered up together

Intruder

diminishing time with you
immobile in your chair
both startled by a
sudden bovine visitor
our breath in-held
what to do?

liquid eyes
gaze large on us
bored she turns
leisurely leaving
expelled breath
becomes hysterical laughter
my father's joins mine
tears course down his cheeks

the comedy of the moment isn't lost
on him nor is his vulnerability

Prayer

head sunken on his chest
his lips moving gently
finger tracing out the words
in a black missal

with physical life greatly diminished
his mind homed in
on the rapture
of each fresh passage
of scripture

….and he felt himself blest

Photos

one image of you

frozen in time
walking up the lane
leaning on your stick
sporting the flat cap
your familiar face
wearing that smile
past farming now
but content to see
all's in order

another photo

head hung down
onto your chest
        frail
            shrunken
Big Peter no longer
in others memory
but in our hearts
                        forever
                              Big Peter

Flight

a bird flew down the chimney
in my parents' room
swooping   disorientated
we ushered it from the window
my father's spirit flying free
it made my mother smile

you knew your time was short
you wanted home those last days
I travelled back in the ambulance
soothing   holding your hand
It won't be long now.
We're at the crossroads

those days at home a constant struggle
a fight for breath painful to hear
amidst sounds of teacups
the news on TV
we sat with you night and day
John did too   so many cups of tea

I went to stay by your side
within minutes
you were gone from me
painful breathing stilled

we readied the house for the wake

a bird flew down the chimney in my parents' room
swooping   disorientated
we ushered it from the window
my father's spirit flying free
it made my mother smile

The Jumper

the jumper was soft and ball-y
stretched at the front
from fitting over his stomach
with frayed cuffs
and holes at the elbows
it still smelt of hay meadows
apple scented tobacco
I wore it as a potent reminder
redolent as it was with every day memories

Charlie

young farmer bred
tractor driving
creating seed beds
nurturing the sod
lookin' the cattle
fodderin' the ewes
birthing new lambs
at age twelve

he's a man child
the innocence of a boy
yet his tongue is salted
with an old countryman's lore

~ and the heart shares ~

Fragility

bleakness blackness
grief
surgery radiotherapy
womanhood taken
alien body

alive

Hugh

The imprint of tragedy upon a family
like Ash Wednesday's anointing
sadness across generations
cruelty of fates
a little brother taken
a young daughter's death
devastating blows
life blasted apart
words wholly inadequate
to convey grief's depths

Stillness

You have to be prepared to lose this child
the midwife's words assaulted my ears
splintered my heart
two of them stayed by my side
holding my hands   murmuring to me
kind words I couldn't take in

a few hours later
a junior doctor arriving
An injection might be the answer
I clung to his words
everything might still work out
he left the room but didn't return

the frustrations of the midwives
as my contractions grew closer together
eventually he returned with the syringe
which he passed over   and left

my legs were clamped together
in fear   dread of this birth
which spelt death -

hope the doctor had ushered in
now ebbed away
as I imagined that little life would -

soon it was over

his little body   lifeless
was placed in my arms
he was beautiful
but his bruised skin
told of a painful journey
in   and   out   of this world

Jack

Touching your black hair
and curled eyelashes
nails like tiny seed pearls
your small body - perfect
only lacking that last
trimester baby fat

in the funeral parlour
watching over you
a sense of peace
in the presence of greatness
at once My Baby
and Guardian Angel

Incantation

you were the first person I told
telephone shrinking
the hundreds of miles
told you how that boy
inside me was gone
came too early to survive

you kept repeating
poor girl, poor girl
like a sorrowful incantation
somehow sound soothed me
enabled telling of my story
without breaking down

You

on dank December anniversaries
flaming like the sparkle of your eyes
the candles soothe and focus me
into memories
recalling the tealights
hanging from your tree
swinging in the wind

in early days of grieving
I saw an image of you
as a small boy
running away from me
face concealed

my thoughts turn to
the life you didn't have
I imagine you
a lively five year old
your wide smile as you race your trains
at ten shimmying up a tree
our lives lit by you

at fifteen spending time
with cousins on the family farm
helping at lambing time
and with the calving

I sit quiet in the candlelight
feeling accommodation
to your loss

~ and the child said ~

The Magic Box

~After Kit Wright~

I will put in the box…

footfalls of angels
tinkling laughter of children
soft strumming of a harp

I will put in the box…

joyful sound of a yodel
leap of a small ballet dancer
fog that rolls across a river

I will put in the box…

an ice maiden dancing in the sun
frown of an old curmudgeon
mermaid wearing a red jumper

I will put in the box…

icy splash of sea on my skin
salmon swimming in honey
mackerel dancing a jig

my box is made from scales shed by snakes
shimmering pink   green and gold
it's handles are jewel encrusted   ancient crab claws

I shall carry my box with care
aboard a sailing ship with a bright green sail
we shall navigate the briny ocean
gliding into a sunset.

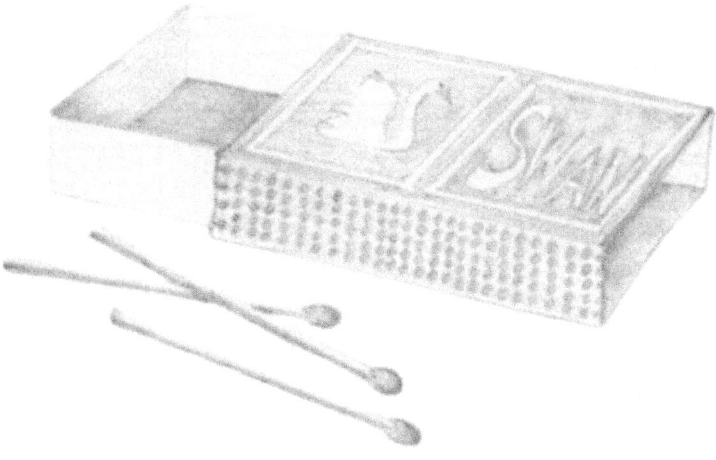

A Watery Adventure

The dusty old book was sitting there just begging to be read. The font was archaic and ornate. The opening letter of each page was surrounded by embossed golden swirls and colourful flowers.

Bobby began to read.

~ ~ ~ ~ ~

Once there was a tiny elf called Jeremiah who lived close to a river. More than anything he loved to walk along the riverbank where he could watch the fishermen, their faces bent over their lines and admire the fat shiny fish as they jumped and somersaulted.

Whatever the weather or the season it looked beautiful. There was always something new to see. Sometimes there would be a family of water birds. Often the mother would carry a fluffy baby on her back. As the sun went down on a summer evening Jeremiah might catch sight of a snowy owl, almost skimming the water as it glided along looking for food.

Jeremiah lived in a broken down old green house. An uncomfortable home, he really wanted to fix it up, but it was so old and Jeremiah was so small, that was difficult. Panes of glass were missing and broken so the wind whistled through. It had the musty smell of the old vegetables which Jeremiah hadn't been able to clear out. The beds in the green house had been taken over by clumps of grass and weeds. now covered in dust and cobwebs like heavy grey curtains.

Belinda the Dormouse also lived in the green house. She had never spoken to Jeremiah and believed it was a secret she was there. Jeremiah played along with this, relieved at not having to talk to her. He never knew what to say to new people. Belinda, an only child and alone in the world, was grateful to share a home with someone else. As a way of saying thanks, she would leave out plates of food for him from time to time. She would have liked to talk to Jeremiah but could tell by watching him that he wasn't one for chatting.

Beside Jeremiah's green house was an abandoned stable. Until recently it had been occupied by a large family of mice but when they moved out into the fields, a young vole called Cynthia moved in. She fancied herself as a singer and practised her songs at all hours of the day and night. Jeremiah had to admit that she was good, but he didn't want to hear constant singing. Summoning all of his courage he knocked on her door. When she answered he asked her politely and timidly if she would stop singing at least at night so that he could get to sleep. Cynthia said no and slammed the door. Back at the green house, Jeremiah berated himself for not being firmer.

Just then there was a knock at the door. It was Jeremiah's brothers asking him to come with them next day on a mountaineering expedition. Immediately Jeremiah turned them down, saying it was too dangerous. The brothers left a short time later, laughing and joking together as usual.

That night there was a ferocious storm. The thunder rumbled, the lightning cracked, the rain beat down and the wind howled through the rickety green house. Jeremiah was wet and cold. When morning came he wasn't surprised to see that most of the remaining panes of glass in the greenhouse now lay broken on the ground.

A bigger shock hit him when he looked out at the stable where Cynthia lived. A large part of her roof was missing where it had been hit by lightning. Seeing Cynthia's back disappearing in the direction of the river, he wondered if she'd gone to find somewhere new to live. Moments later he saw Belinda walking briskly along the same path. He felt sad, and then surprised, as he realized he would miss her. As often happens, a beautiful golden sunny day unfolded after the storm of the night before. Jeremiah knew he needed to find somewhere to live but felt it would be a shame to waste the sunshine. The river, his favourite walk, called to him.

Belinda was indeed walking along the riverbank searching for a new home. Sniffing the air and ground as she walked, she spied a burrow. Unsure if it was being used, she rather nervously went deep down into it to check it out. Her nose told her it had definitely belonged to a badger, but the scent was faint, leading her to believe that it had been empty for some time. It had three large rooms, each one opening off the other. Wondering whether to fill the space or just enjoy the emptiness, in the end, she felt it needed a few personal touches to make it feel like her home. She decided to continue her walk along the riverbank to see what she could find to put in it.

The first find, washed up on the gravelly bank, was a small bottle, a wonderful shade of green with pretty decorations. As the bottle would make a lovely vase. she dragged it back along the bank to the empty badger sett. Passing a clump of buttercups beside the path she thought how lovely they would look in her vase. Gathering a large armful of them, she arranged them in the bottle with great care. With their delicate scent filling her new living room, the last of the badger scent was gone.

After a few minutes admiring the floral display, she scampered back out of the burrow along the riverbank. She took in the sights and sounds as she bounded along. A large beautifully painted barge chugging along, fishermen in waders boldly striding into the river as they flicked their rods, elves and rodents going about their business.

Suddenly she heard a high-pitched scream, a cry for help. She recognised the voice from the nighttime singing. It was Cynthia. Surfing on a piece of bark in the river, not realising how fast it was moving after the heavy rain of the previous night, the young vole found herself crashing into other animals and river users. From the path where he had been watching Belinda's activities, Jeremiah took in the scene at a glance.

Without a moment's hesitation he dived into the

river. Perhaps Belinda could help too. She ran along the bank trying to keep pace with Jeremiah. Meanwhile the river continued to carry Cynthia forward at speed, pushing her first against the bank, then back into the centre of the river again. The sight of Jeremiah coming to rescue her quietened her cries for help until the river once again took control of her fragile piece of bark. Cries of alarm filled the air again. Jeremiah swam faster than he'd ever done before.

Meanwhile Belinda ran along the bank panting furiously but determined to be of help. Inch by inch Jeremiah gained ground on Cynthia. With a mighty push he caught up with her, took hold of the bark and gently steered it towards the bank where Belinda was waiting with open paws. A rescued Cynthia clung to her, crying, and laughing with joy, relieved her ordeal was at an end.

By the time Jeremiah stepped out on to the bank a crowd was waiting to greet him, clapping and cheering, calling him a hero. Smiling with shy delight, he turned to Belinda.

You're Belinda, aren't you? I know you from the green house. Belinda looked surprised. I didn't think you knew I was there.

I suspected that but I didn't mind. There was plenty of space for both of us. Belinda felt her cheeks go pink. We need to get this young one home, she flustered.

She doesn't have a home, none of us do.

I think I might have solved that problem for us all. Follow me. I'll show you.

Jeremiah bent down and put Cynthia on his back while Belinda walked by his side. On reaching the burrow. Belinda climbed down into it, encouraging the others to follow her.

We can have a room each, she said with warm enthusiasm.

I'd love to share this burrow with you both. I promise I'd be much more considerate when I sing, begged Cynthia.

I'd like to stay too, Jeremiah confessed to Belinda and Cynthia.

A very happy Belinda was over-joyed. At last, this only child, alone in the world, had found herself a family.

When Jeremiah's brothers returned from their day of climbing, they learnt about the broken green house and of Jeremiah's daring rescue of Cynthia. They hugged him, telling him how proud they were, how delighted they were he would not be on his own anymore. He'd always been different from them. Now all the brothers were content, more like each other than they had ever been before.

Bobby closed the book with a smile.

Hortense the Giraffe

The dusty old book was sitting there just begging to be read. The font was archaic and ornate. The opening letter of each page was surrounded by embossed golden swirls and colourful flowers.

~ ~ ~ ~ ~

Bobby began to read about a sad giraffe called Hortense. She had a broken leg and to add to her troubles she was struggling with a damaged wooden crutch.

Hortense couldn't balance and stretch to eat the succulent leaves from the top of the trees and had to make do with the bitter tasting bottom ones.

She felt lonely, missing out on the family walks. In the distance all of them could see lions stretched out in the shade of trees. The birds of prey perched in the top most branches suddenly taking off hunting.

She couldn't skip and frolic with her friends and stood forlornly as they laughed and chased each other.

Tears ran down Hortense's long dark eye lashes. How could she hope to get around with a wrecked crutch? Life seemed just impossible.

Suddenly a ball of brightly coloured light danced in front of her eyes. As she looked it became still and out of it jumped a dainty fairy.

Nothing is ever truly impossible she said. *I can help by granting you a wish.*

The giraffe smiled. *Can you heal my broken leg?*
Of course the fairy tinkled.

She waved her wand over the giraffe. There was a small puff of smoke and Hortense looked down at her set of four perfect legs. Did she imagine it? She felt stronger and fitter than ever before. She jumped and twirled in a circle calling out her *thank-yous* to the fairy as she did so.

Bobby closed the book with a smile.

The Elf on the Shelf

The dusty old book was sitting there, just begging to be read. The font was archaic and ornate. The opening letter of each page was surrounded by embossed golden swirls and colourful flowers.

Bobby began to read.

~ ~ ~ ~ ~

The berries on the holly wreath were wizened, the leaves brown and crunchy. Unhooked from the front door it went in to the compost bin.

Decorations taken down, a faded area of paintwork was revealed. Carrie folded away the artificial tree. Baubles, strings of shining tinsel and fairy lights were packed. It brought a lump to her throat to see the house, it seemed lonely, forlorn and abandoned.

Just one decoration left. Seated on the mantelpiece was the elf. Clad entirely in red – tunic, tights and lace trimmed cap, his slim legs dangling, his feet in wooden clogs.

She thought of leaving him there for company, but

worried it might be unlucky, so he too was packed away. It felt like losing a friend.

The elf lay flat in the cardboard box, claustrophobic in the darkness. He didn't relish the prospect of being confined for another year.

He remembered with fondness his place on the mantelpiece. The woman wrote stories and poetry and he could listen as she read her work aloud. *How to break out of this prison?* Raising his legs and pushing the lid of the box with his feet, but feeling only the tiniest movement. Keeping going until tired and shaky.

The lead soldiers had watched his struggle. The captain called them to attention and they formulated an escape plan for the elf. It was agreed that two of the most athletic soldiers would act as a climbing frame. Another would give the elf a leg up until he stood with a foot on each man's shoulder.

The plan was speedily executed. The elf now much closer to the lid could push with his shoulders and hands. Soon he had succeeded in pushing it clear and scrambling down the side, calling a cheery *Thank you* to his helpers. Once outside his normal powers were restored and he wasted no time in flying to the living room. Resuming his position, legs crossed. When Carrie came downstairs next morning she saw him straight away. She was startled.

I could have sworn I'd packed you away

She reached out to pick him up, then noticed his crossed legs.

Your legs were definitely dangling before

He winked at her from his black right eye. She shook her head in disbelief, so he winked at her again. She laughed

I think you're my lucky elf. You can stay.

Bobby closed the book with a smile.

The Stone Seal

The dusty old book was sitting there just begging to be read. The font was archaic and ornate. The opening letter of each page was surrounded by embossed golden swirls and colourful flowers.

Bobby began to read.

~ ~ ~ ~ ~

The stone seal sat on his plinth on the promenade. He gazed down to the beach, listening to laughter and watching the sea- seals at play. They basked on rocks with the hot sun soaking into their glistening skin. The mother nuzzled her pups with love, played tumble with them in the waves.

He felt like an outsider a hidden observer. His days were spent watching the lives of the sea- seals as they lived loved laughed. Sometimes he was able to take pleasure in their happiness. At other times he felt a weight of sadness in his stone heart that he could never be part of their lives. At these times he would have cried.

He tried to console himself that he had an eternity on the Earth whereas the other seals only had a short time. But he knew that he was fooling himself. Through giving birth and rearing strong beautiful pups the seals had a claim to eternity. His existence felt like a curse. The more he watched the seals the more his sense of loss and longing deepened yet he found it impossible to ignore them.

The stone seal slept. He had a powerful dream in which he came to life. He delighted in basking in the warm sun diving through the waves. In his dream he found a soulmate with whom to have a family of sleek healthy pups. When she birthed the pups he was the proudest father in the world.

Once awake the dream's imprint was still upon him. That moment of bittersweetness. The next morning, a mother and child passed the stone seal.

Look the seal's crying mummy.
Don't be silly stone seals can't cry.
He looks happy though.

Bobby closed the book with a smile.

An Unlikely Hero

The dusty old book was sitting there just begging to be read. The font was archaic and ornate. The opening letter of each page was surrounded by embossed golden swirls and colourful flowers.

Bobby began to read.

~ ~ ~ ~ ~

The draft excluder dog lay to the side of the door. He often felt like sneezing because of the dust and fluff gathering in his nostrils. He had to stifle the urge because he knew it would startle the family to see him sneeze.

At times he felt lonely. It appeared that they were blind to his existence. Soon it would be Winter. The father would pick him up plonk him down at the base of the living room door. His poor bruised body would absorb the drafts created by the wind while the family gathered around the fire. He appreciated that he was useful but struggled with seeming to be invisible.

One night everyone had gone to bed. About to doze off the window creaked open. A man climbed in dressed in dark clothes and gloves carrying a large holdall. He began to lift valuables and stow them in the bag.

The dog felt the velour on his neck rise up. His mind raced with thoughts of how to catch the burglar. When the man came near him the dog sprang forward clamping his teeth around his ankle. The man yelped in pain and shock at seeing the draft excluder come to life. He tripped and banged his head collapsing on the hearth.

The dog now began to bark loudly. The whole family came to investigate. Imagine their shock. A burglar knocked out on the floor. The draft excluder dog stood guard over him. Mr Grey the children's father, immediately phoned for the police. They arrived within minutes quickly handcuffing the still dazed burglar.

The children picked up the dog. They gathered around the embers taking it in turn to praise him and stroke his soft coat. The dog felt he was wrapped in the family's love.

At last he truly belonged.

Bobby closed the book with a smile.

The Amazing Abel Starlight

The dusty old book was sitting there just begging to be read. The font was archaic and ornate. The opening letter of each page was surrounded by embossed golden swirls and colourful flowers.

Bobby began to read. He knew these characters now

~ ~ ~ ~ ~

Jeremiah, the youngest of the elf family, had been feeling guilty about not seeing his family for a long time. With such a busy life it was easy to get caught up in his own concerns. For his brothers and parents, it was exactly the same. Although they lived close by they were all so busy that sometimes weeks might go by without a proper chat. Also, worried that they might not like him living with a dormouse and a vole, he hadn't yet invited them round to see his new home.

Walking through the woods on his way to visit them, he spotted a thrush's egg lying at the bottom of a tree. It wasn't broken or even cracked, and still felt warm. Looking up through the branches for a nest, there was no sign of either a mother or father bird. Jeremiah knew it was important to keep the egg warm. Carefully climbing onto it, he spread out his arms and legs and tried to remain still for what seemed like hours. Eventually he fell asleep, dreaming that he was struggling to feed a baby bird. Waking with a stiff neck, and no sign of any returning parent birds, he began to wonder what he'd taken on. How was he going to keep the egg warm? How was he going to feed the baby bird when it hatched?

Much to his surprise, his brother Jason, out for a morning stroll, appeared on the path beside the tree. Explaining the situation to him, he asked if he'd mind taking over for an hour so that he could stretch his legs and get something to eat.

Of course I will. Why don't you ask the twins Jack and John for help as well?

Waiting until Jason was balanced on the egg Jeremiah strode off in the direction of his parents' house, stretching his arms and rolling his head back and forth to ease the stiffness in his neck. On walking through the door, he saw a pot of dandelion stew bubbling on the stove, the delicious smell making him realise how hungry he was.

His mother's eyes widened in wonder as he told her about his find over a bowl of the tasty stew.

Jason's right. We must all take turns in helping to keep the egg warm.

After eating, he went in search of Jack and John. Soon, between them, they worked out a rota for the next few days when they would each care for the egg. While they were all excited, they did wonder how long it would be before it hatched, and felt equally anxious about how they'd feed the baby bird.

Jeremiah went back to the burrow which he shared with Belinda the dormouse and Cynthia the vole. When he told them the whole story they too were keen to help in some way. Patting her tummy Belinda feared she might too heavy to lie on top of the egg.

I could help by bringing you all food and drink while you're keeping it warm.

She was delighted at the thought of making delicious snacks and cakes to keep everyone well fed.

Several days went by with Belinda cooking wonderful delights for the elves and Cynthia as they kept the egg warm. Belinda and Cynthia enjoyed the company of the young elves. Both now loved Jeremiah dearly, but he was often serious whereas his brothers were funny and light-hearted.

Finally, the day they'd been waiting for arrived. Shortly into his early shift one morning, Jeremiah heard a hammering coming from inside the egg. Carefully sliding off it, he lowered himself to the ground. A sudden explosion of shell! A shocked Jeremiah saw a tiny bare-chested man carrying a lamp stride out of the shell ruins. He was very muscular, with purple satin trousers ballooning out around his legs, golden pumps curling upwards on his feet and a colourful turban swathing his head.

You're a genie, cried Jeremiah with delight.

The small man bowed low. *I am The Amazing Abel Starlight,* he said in an intriguing accent. *I was captured by the powerful Fernando, an evil genie who trapped me inside the egg. Without the kindness of you, your family and friends I wouldn't have survived.*

Jeremiah was embarrassed and shuffled his feet, but the genie continued to speak.

I can reward you all by giving you one wish which you must share. You have twelve hours in which to unanimously agree upon your wish. After that time my power to grant it will disappear. I will give you my lamp. When you've agreed on which wish to choose, rub the lamp three times and I will re-appear.

Picking up the lamp while thanking Abel, Jeremiah walked home. As it was only 7am Belinda and Cynthia were just getting up, rubbing sleep from their eyes. When he told them of the events of the last hour, they were speechless with amazement. Inviting them to his family's home, the three of them set off. Once there the elven family listened with fascination as Jeremiah told them about the genie and the wish.

The twins Jack and John announced at the exact same time that they wanted to meet someone with whom they could fall in love.

That's all very well, said their father, *but it doesn't give the rest of us anything.*

The twins looked very disappointed.

The boys' father now spoke up. He said that he would like a second home by the sea where they could all go for holidays. They could lie on the warm golden sand and listen to the sounds of the sea. His wife and the boys liked the idea but none of them felt it was the thing they most wanted.

Jeremiah, a keen cyclist, said he would like to win a medal in the Olympic Games. He acknowledged sadly, however, that, like the twins wish, it didn't reward anyone else.

The boys' mother said she'd like a big motor car so that they could all go exploring wherever they liked. They could camp out or just sleep in the car. Again, the elven family liked the suggestion in general but, as they each had their own ideas they didn't want to commit to it.

Belinda spoke of a cookery school and Cynthia of a concert hall where bands could play. Jack, a committed book worm, said he'd like a lifetimes' supply of books. The others groaned loudly.

The debate went on through the morning with different ideas bouncing back and forth. They grew tired of it. By lunchtime everyone, apart from the elves' mother, was asleep. She had passed the morning preparing a buttercup casserole, feeling very satisfied when she saw it bubbling in the oven, but then she too fell asleep.

Jeremiah woke first, noting with shock that it was almost 5 o'clock in the evening. There were only two hours left for the wish to be granted. He quickly woke everyone. Agreeing that they needed to eat first, they settled down to enjoy the casserole. Afterwards they returned to the lively debate. With only half an hour left they realized with frustration that they were going round in circles.

Suddenly Jeremiah gave a cheer. *I have it,* he said. *Why don't we ask for the One Special Wish which will make us all happy, but we will leave the choice of it up to Abel the Genie.*

Jeremiah's family, Cynthia and Belinda gathered round him, clapping him warmly on the back, saying what an excellent idea this was. Jeremiah rubbed the lamp three times. With a sudden puff of smoke, the genie appeared.

I'm pleased to meet you he said bowing low to the family of elves, Belinda and Cynthia. *Have you agreed upon a wish*?

We want whatever will make us all happy, stated Jeremiah.

The genie smiled. *A wise decision. You will receive your wish within the next week.*

Another puff of smoke and the genie vanished.

The elves, Cynthia and Belinda cheered, hugged, and kissed each other, excited at the thought of what the next week might bring. Jeremiah suggested they should meet regularly to report to each other anything which might show that the wish had been granted. They would need to keep an eye out for anything unusual. The elves, Belinda and Cynthia decided to meet for dinner each evening to compare notes. Each night after discussing the wish first, they could spend the rest of the time sharing the news of their day.

By the end of the week, they were closer than they'd ever been. Even better as now Cynthia and Belinda were part of the family, included in everything which the elves did. Jeremiah realized he should not have doubted his parents. They always accepted everyone. However, no new motor car or second home or life supply of books had appeared. On the face of it nothing had changed, yet each of them said they had never felt happier. They hugged each other regularly with delight at how good they were feeling.

At dinner on the last evening of the week of waiting for their Special Wish to appear, Jack, a deeper thinker than the others, suggested that all along, they'd had everything they needed to be happy. Perhaps being together, enjoying each other's company was enough. The elven family, Cynthia and Belinda showed their agreement with a loud cheer, sharing a warm hug among each other. Abel had granted their wish indeed! They were truly the happiest they'd ever been.

Bobby closed the book with a smile.

Kiss Chase

in the *Girls* playground singing
...in and out go the dusty bluebells..

on impulse I'm seized and bundled
through the gate
to where the *Boys* play
grabbed in a clumsy hug by Sam
he plants a gloopy kiss on my eye brow
I watch the colour rise in childish cheeks
know my face echoes his
a chivalrous favour bestowed

with awkward haste I'm pitched back
into skipping ropes and girlish games

War

nine years of age   flush with importance
looking after granny for the summer
granda   gone to Heaven at Easter

eight years of age a cousin sharing the load
hating me for getting in her way
I was here first

brother and sisters left at home
were replaced with new play mates
            cousins living up the lane

1973   helicopters circled   hovered
playing at our *War* we launched ourselves
onto sand piles like great actors

at night forgetting window – dizzy moths
I buried my face in the eiderdown
fearing the flutter of furry bodies on a cheek

Closeness

hands touching as we patted the castle
walking side by side carrying water for the moat
finding an easy rhythm sculpting with our fingers
digging and smoothing and filling
occasionally heads brushing together
concentrating on tasks
air between us humming
with joy of a shared venture

Russell Park, London

~ a water fountain ~

droplets bead on
faces turned upwards
children chasing
slithering   sliding
clothes glued to bodies
hands extended
plashing the others
laughter like a musical
or fox cubs at play
four of them   to and fro
wetter and wetter
each outdoing the other

onlookers smile   laugh
some mesmerised
childhood memories stirred
envying vibrant youth
longing to join
but self-conscious

responsible adult syndrome

Skipping

at home I skipped alone
in school we took turns
to twirl the rope
faster   and faster   ever faster
to the words of well-worn songs
now faded in my memory
the rhythm alone stays with me
a magical metronome of foot falls
marching a military tattoo
our girlish voices
keeping time   beating time
with our feet

Disco

Bra stuffed with tissues
in my lumber shirt
and skin tight jeans
I sashay across tiles, jumping
as electrifying sounds of
I feel love fill floor
girls crowd together
dancing self-consciously
high pitched laughter exaggerated
boys stand on side lines
practising air of coolness
each seem to orbit other
experiencing gravitational pull
when lights go down
and it's time for slow numbers

Butterfly

It's only a little bit dead
Put it in the sun. It might get better
with soft leaves   blades of grass   moss
the painstaking construction of a stretcher
where a butterfly could heal
it was carried with tenderness into the warmth

respectful waiting began
but it remained prone
on its funereal bower
It's not gonna get better
their little faces were grave
life was less carefree that day
for that innocent cortege

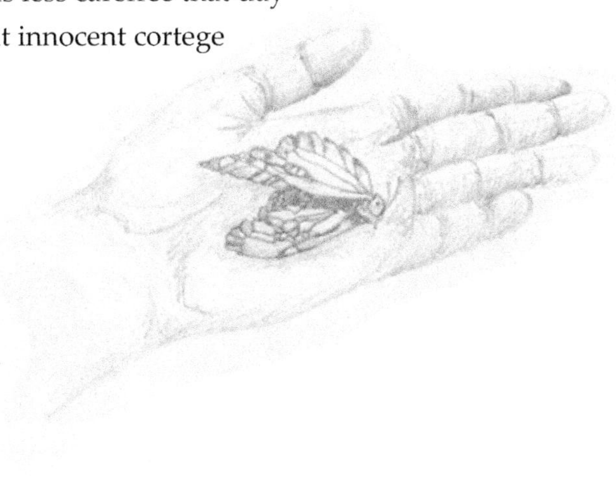

The Magic Box (II)

~ after Kit Wright ~

I will put in the box…

a batik cloth reflecting sunlight
raindrops from my collection
the blink of an eye

I will put in the box…

an elf from outer space
three wishes granted by a pirate
a bluebell growing in a snowdrift

I will put in the box…

a dolphin in a denim jacket
spindrift from a wave
a ladybird's footprints

I will put in the box…

the smile of a rattlesnake
a fairy whooshing on a skateboard
a snowflake bouncing on a trampoline

the box is made of wind scattered petals
it opens to accommodate treasures
its hinges are four words of kindness

I shall float in my box
drifting in the cobalt waves
then come ashore on an icy island
where polar bears romp and play

~ afterwords ~

Balm

(for Roisin)

fingers caressing plants
breaking off a leaf of mint
chewing it, reflecting
that senses are soothed

each inch of embankment claimed
garden colours blur
for those on whizzing trains
mindful weeding
blesses this place
gifting freedom
from daily demands

courgettes rub shoulders
with pansies and fuchsia
pots of all hues splatter
a greenhouse where
tomato scents infuse the air
and growing salad leaves
delicately dance

stolen moments

Zendo

Wapp of wood on wood
a summons to Zendo
rustling robes
they file into their spaces
breathing a range of rhythms
into the air

A gong sounds - its music
a continuous   shimmering haze
announces Kinhin
chanting   rich and mellow follows
incense pungent in the sound
they sit: come face to face
with themselves

Saving

I save the imprint of your body
on the mattress
the damp corner of the towel
where you dried your face
I save the dent in the cushion
where you sprawled luxuriously
to watch TV

I save the coffee
in the bottom of your cup
which your lips have brushed
I save the spot on the carpet
where you stood to kiss me
I save all of these
and more

everything your body has touched

Synaestheses

Anger

tastes like a burnt potato from the fire's embers
anger sounds like a tuneless orchestra
anger looks like a fight outside the pub
anger smells like blood from a stab wound
anger feels like powerlessness against injustice

Inspiration

looks like an exquisite sunrise
inspiration sounds like a violin concerto
inspiration feels like the grace of a ballet dancer
inspiration tastes like an exotic cocktail
inspiration smells like a heady perfume

Happiness

tastes like Rum'n' Raisin ice cream
happiness smells like wild roses in a meadow
happiness sounds like the clapping of hands
happiness looks like a gurgling baby
happiness feels like a fluffy mallow teacake

Sadness

smells like a dead fire's ashes
sadness feels like broken glass in a photo frame
sadness sounds like a tolling funeral bell
sadness tastes like salt tears
sadness looks like a starving child

senses swirl in synaesthesia

Transition

In the woods Autumn
will soon take its leave
and Winter will hold sway
now   trees in red   yellow   orange
dry   crisp   rustling
like wedding petticoats
and overhead a raw raucous of rooks

wafer crunching leaves
tell an autumnal tale
mulched underfoot
they speak of Winter's
imminent arrival
laying waste to trees
leaving black skeletons

after…
pondering transition
oblivious to harsh beauty
of those denuded trees
not seeing a season's sad glamour
quiescence for Nature
shivering through it
wanting it to end

I Don't Really Need You Now

I don't really need you now
what of your infectious laughter?
what of your twinkling eyes?

I don't really need you now
what of your lithe, agile body?
what of your boyish grin?

I don't really need you now
what of the funny things you say?
what of your beautiful, graceful hands?

I don't really need you now
what of the lightness of your kiss?
what of lying in your arms?

I don't really need you now
I don't really need you now

Let There Be Laughter

~After Lemn Sissay~

let there be laughter
so smiles open themselves as wide as the sky
and snails pole vault in the Olympic Games
so undertakers become ballroom dancers
and strong men practice ballet
in fluffy pink tutus

let there be laughter
so waves still
and chuckle at the moon
so the piglet and hedgehog swim with dolphins
let the young French woman pirouetting
on top of a large cream cake
become a live decoration

let there be laughter
let tears on the cheeks of children
be dried by a caressing breeze
let waves kiss the shore
with smiling mouths
let harsh words explode
into fragments of coloured glass
tumbling to Earth in technicolour showers

Twenty-one

heady student days
a summer job in Jersey
first earnings used to buy
a backless   white jump suit
at 21 it was the last word in
sophistication

my cousin's wedding reception
the perfect occasion
ravishing in my outfit
attracting lustful stares
from a guest old
enough to be my dad…
so not my type

the evening wasted
in a bid to escape
orbiting constantly orbiting
the dance floor
Help spinning in my head.

for years a banished jump suit
languished in the wardrobe

I Come From

(after Robert Seatter)

I come from Coolnasillagh
behind the sallies
where rain rain   rain falls
greening the fields
and we play in snow drifts
I come from hay fields
with fragrant meadow sweet
and curlew call
from the Moss
where the turf is cut
curing in the sunshine
and summer breeze

I come from Belfast
I come from care-free
student days
enjoying the craic
in the Empire Bar
Lavery's and the Limelight
sharing a flat with friends
bantering over who uses
the most electricity

I come from Stanstead in Suffolk
from walks in barley and rape fields
enjoying the shade of woods
in the heat of the summer
listening out for the nightingale
I come from the sea
from icy dips
and walks on the shore
drinking sights and sounds
writing down sensations

Acknowledgements of First Publication

Menopausal Mermaids (November, December) were published in *Irish Hares and Seahorses,* Impspired.com, 2022

Menopausal Mermaids (January) was published in Poetry in Motion, Community Arts Partnership, *Heartland*, 2021

Murmuration was published in *Woven Words and Spun Tales,* Impspired.com, 2023

Today I Miss the Sea was published in *Woven Words and Spun Tales,* Impspired.com, 2023

Milking Time was published in *Spindrift,* an anthology from Portrush Writers, 2018

The Tilley Lamp was published in *Spindrift,* an anthology from Portrush Writers, 2018

Ageing was published in *Reeling In,* an anthology from Portrush Writers, 2021

Byre was published in *Reeling In,* an anthology from Portrush Writers, 2021

Grain of Sand was published in Poetry in Motion, Community Arts Partnership Anthology, *Heartland,* 2021

Prayer was published in *Irish Hares and Seahorses,* Impspired.com, 2022

Flight was published in *Spindrift,* an anthology from Portrush Writers, 2018

Stillness was published in *Love, Loss and Cardiac Issues,* Impspired.com, 2022

Incantation was published in *Woven Words and Spun Tales,* Impspired.com, 2023

The Magic Box was published in the online magazine *Sage Cigarettes.com,* 2022

The Elf on the Shelf was published in *Woven Words and Spun Tales,* Impspired.com, 2023

Closeness was published in *Reeling In,* an anthology from Portrush Writers, 2021

Skipping was published in *Reeling In,* an anthology from Portrush Writers, 2021

Butterfly was published in *Spindrift,* an anthology from Portrush Writers, 2018

The Magic Box II was published in *Poetry in Motion,* Community Arts Partnership, Compass, 2022/23

Balm was published in *Irish Hares and Seahorses,* Impspired.com, 2022

Synaestheses was published in *Irish Hares and Sea Horses,* Impspired.com, 2022

Let there be Laughter was published in *Spindrift* an anthology from Portrush Writers, 2018

Notes

Menopausal Mermaids -
is the name of the group of women sea swimmers which Sinéad Coxhill belongs to.

Portrush in Autumn -
Portrush is the name of the seaside town where Sinéad Coxhill lives.

Murmuration -
Starlings fly in huge numbers. A murmuration is the sound made by their wings.

Scene of Crime -
is about a tern which was the victim of Avian Influenza (bird flu)

The Tilley Lamp -
During World War I Tilley Lamps were used by the British armed forces. They became so popular in many parts of the Commonwealth that Tilley became used as a generic name for a paraffin lamp.

The Ritual -

The midden is an area on a farm where animal waste and household food waste are deposited. Once rotted down it is spread on the land as a fertiliser.

Turas Deireanach -

is Irish for 'final journey'

Lough Derg -

is a place of pilgrimage. Time there is spent in prayer and fasting. On arrival on the island pilgrims remove their shoes and socks. They only put these on again when they have completed the pilgrimage. On the first night they must stay awake, on the second they sleep in basic dormitories. Much of the prayer takes place outside, walking barefoot over stones.

Charlie -

lookin' - checking that the livestock are all present, safe and well. fodderin'- bringing hay and feed to the cattle/ sheep in the fields.

Zendo -

is a hall where Zen Buddhists practice formal seated meditation (Zazen) Kinhin is walking meditation.

About the Author

Sinéad Coxhill grew up on a farm in Northern Ireland. She studied English at Queen's University Belfast and Social Work at the University of Ulster Jordanstown. She worked in social work for five years before moving to England where she trained as an art therapist, working in art therapy for seven years. She lived on a small holding in Suffolk with her now ex-husband where they reared rare breed pigs and grew their own vegetables.
She has been living in Northern Ireland since 2013, settling in the north coast town of Portrush.
She began writing poetry in 2014. Her work was supported and encouraged by Kate Murphy, facilitator of Portrush Writers and by Mary Farrell, facilitator of North Coast Writers.
In 2016, her poem *Milking Time* was selected by Waterstones, Coleraine as part of a month-long display of poems for International Women's Day.
In 2018 she toured parts of England, performing in open mics. In 2019 she performed at Waterstones in Birmingham as part of a group of English and Northern Irish poets. In 2019 she also performed at the Red Sails and Stendhal Festivals in Northern Ireland. In 2022 she performed at the Abbey Lane Theatre, Armagh in Northern Ireland.
In 2022 she won a bursary to attend the John Hewitt

Literary Arts Festival and Summer School in Armagh. She found this a great experience in terms of workshopping, being exposed to the work of new and established writers and making contacts with peers on the summer school. She had a dream of publishing a collection of her poetry and in 2022 began working towards making this a reality.

Printed in Great Britain
by Amazon

29849583R10076